Soups & Stews

Table of Contents

Beef 'n' Pork

beefy broccoli & cheese soup

¼ pound ground beef

2 cups beef broth

1 package (10 ounces) frozen chopped broccoli, thawed

¼ cup chopped onion

1 cup milk

2 tablespoons all-purpose flour

1 cup (4 ounces) shredded sharp Cheddar cheese

1½ teaspoons chopped fresh oregano *or* ½ teaspoon dried oregano

Salt and black pepper

Hot pepper sauce

1. Brown beef in large nonstick skillet over medium-high heat 6 to 8 minutes, stirring to break up meat. Drain fat.

2. Bring broth to a boil in medium saucepan over high heat. Add broccoli and onion; cook 5 minutes or until broccoli is tender. Stir milk into flour in small bowl until smooth. Stir milk mixture and ground beef into saucepan; cook and stir until mixture is thickened and heated through.

3. Add cheese and oregano; stir until cheese is melted. Season with salt, black pepper and hot pepper sauce.

Makes 4 servings

jerk pork and sweet potato stew

　2 tablespoons all-purpose flour
　¼ teaspoon salt
　¼ teaspoon black pepper
1¼ pounds pork shoulder, cut into bite-size pieces
　2 tablespoons vegetable oil
　1 large sweet potato, peeled and diced
　1 cup corn
　4 tablespoons minced green onions, divided
　1 clove garlic, minced
　½ medium Scotch bonnet chile or jalapeño pepper,*
　　　cored, seeded and minced
　⅛ teaspoon ground allspice
　1 cup chicken broth
　1 tablespoon lime juice
　2 cups hot cooked rice

Scotch bonnet chiles and jalapeño peppers can sting and irritate the skin, so wear rubber gloves when handling and do not touch your eyes.

Slow Cooker Directions

1. Combine flour, salt and pepper in large resealable food storage bag. Add pork; shake well to coat. Heat oil in large skillet over medium heat. Working in batches, add pork in single layer and brown on all sides, about 5 minutes. Transfer to slow cooker.

2. Add sweet potato, corn, 2 tablespoons green onions, garlic, chile and allspice. Stir in broth. Cover; cook on LOW 5 to 6 hours.

3. Stir in lime juice and remaining 2 tablespoons green onions. Serve with rice.   **Makes 4 servings**

Prep Time: 15 minutes
Cook Time: 5 to 6 hours

jerk pork and sweet potato stew

beef barley soup

Nonstick cooking spray

¾ pound boneless beef top round steak, trimmed and cut into ½-inch pieces

3 cans (about 14 ounces each) beef broth

1 can (about 14 ounces) diced tomatoes

1 large potato, unpeeled and cut into ½-inch cubes

1 cup chopped onion

1 cup sliced carrots

½ cup uncooked pearl barley

1 tablespoon cider vinegar

2 teaspoons caraway seeds

2 teaspoons dried marjoram

2 teaspoons dried thyme

½ teaspoon salt

½ teaspoon black pepper

1½ cups sliced green beans

1. Spray large saucepan with cooking spray; heat over medium heat. Add beef; cook and stir until browned on all sides.

2. Stir in broth, tomatoes, potato, onion, carrots, barley, vinegar, caraway seeds, marjoram, thyme, salt and pepper; bring to a boil over high heat. Reduce heat to low; cover and simmer 2 hours or until beef is fork-tender, uncovering saucepan and adding green beans during last 30 minutes of cooking.

Makes 4 servings

beef barley soup

mushroom-beef stew

1 pound beef stew meat
1 can (10¾ ounces) condensed cream of mushroom soup, undiluted
2 cans (4 ounces each) sliced mushrooms, drained
1 package (1 ounce) dry onion soup mix
Hot cooked noodles

Slow Cooker Directions

1. Combine beef, condensed soup, mushrooms and soup mix in slow cooker. Cover; cook on LOW 8 to 10 hours.

2. Serve over noodles.   **Makes 4 servings**

long soup

1½ tablespoons vegetable oil
¼ small head cabbage, shredded
8 ounces boneless lean pork, cut into thin strips
6 cups chicken broth
2 tablespoons soy sauce
½ teaspoon minced fresh ginger
8 green onions, cut diagonally into ½-inch slices
4 ounces uncooked Chinese-style thin egg noodles

1. Heat oil in wok or large skillet over medium-high heat. Add cabbage and pork; stir-fry 5 minutes or until pork is barely pink in center.

2. Add broth, soy sauce and ginger; bring to a boil. Reduce heat to low; simmer 10 minutes, stirring occasionally. Stir in green onions. Add noodles; cook 2 to 4 minutes or until noodles are tender.   **Makes 4 servings**

mushroom-beef stew

new mexican green chile pork stew

1½ pounds boneless pork shoulder, cut into 1-inch cubes
2 medium baking potatoes or sweet potatoes, peeled and cut into large chunks
1 cup chopped onion
1 can (4 ounces) diced green chiles
1 cup frozen corn
1 jar (16 ounces) salsa verde (green salsa)
2 teaspoons sugar
2 teaspoons ground cumin or chili powder
1 teaspoon dried oregano
Hot cooked rice
¼ cup chopped fresh cilantro (optional)

Slow Cooker Directions

1. Place pork, potatoes, onion, chiles and corn in slow cooker. Combine salsa, sugar, cumin and oregano in small bowl. Pour over pork and vegetables; stir gently to mix.

2. Cover; cook on LOW 6 to 8 hours or on HIGH 4 to 5 hours. Serve stew with rice; garnish with cilantro.   **Makes 6 servings**

Prep Time: 15 minutes
Cook Time: 6 to 8 hours (LOW) or 4 to 5 hours (HIGH)

new mexican green chile pork stew

kansas city steak soup

½ pound ground beef
3 cups frozen mixed vegetables
2 cups water
1 can (about 14 ounces) stewed tomatoes
1 cup chopped onion
1 cup sliced celery
1 beef bouillon cube
½ to 1 teaspoon black pepper
1 can (about 14 ounces) beef broth
½ cup all-purpose flour

1. Brown beef in large saucepan over medium-high heat 6 to 8 minutes, stirring to break up meat. Drain fat.

2. Add mixed vegetables, water, tomatoes, onion, celery, bouillon cube and pepper to saucepan; bring to a boil.

3. Stir broth into flour in small bowl until smooth. Add to beef mixture; stir until blended. Bring to a boil. Reduce heat to medium-low; cover and simmer 15 minutes, stirring frequently.

Makes 6 servings

tip

If time allows, simmer this soup an additional 30 minutes to further blend the flavors.

kansas city steak soup

spicy pork stew with veggies

    1 teaspoon olive oil
1½ pounds boneless pork loin, trimmed and cut into
        ½-inch cubes
    2 red bell peppers, cut into ¼-inch pieces
    1 large onion, chopped
    1 container (8 ounces) sliced mushrooms
    1 medium acorn squash, peeled and cut into ½-inch
        cubes
    1 can (about 14 ounces) diced tomatoes
    1 can (about 14 ounces) chicken broth
    ½ teaspoon red pepper flakes
    ½ teaspoon black pepper
    ½ teaspoon dried thyme
        Fresh oregano (optional)

1. Heat oil in Dutch oven over medium-high heat. Add half of pork; cook until browned, about 5 minutes, stirring occasionally. Repeat with remaining pork.

2. Add bell peppers, onion and mushrooms to Dutch oven. Stir in squash, tomatoes, broth, red pepper flakes, black pepper and thyme; bring to a boil over high heat. Cover; reduce heat and simmer 1 hour or until pork is tender. Garnish with oregano.

Makes 8 servings

spicy pork stew with veggies

country sausage and bean soup

2 cans (about 14 ounces each) chicken broth
1½ cups hot water
1 cup dried black beans, rinsed and sorted
1 cup chopped yellow onion
2 bay leaves
⅛ teaspoon ground red pepper
6 ounces bulk pork sausage
1 cup chopped tomato
1 tablespoon chili powder
1 tablespoon Worcestershire sauce
2 teaspoons olive oil
1½ teaspoons ground cumin
½ teaspoon salt
¼ cup chopped fresh cilantro

Slow Cooker Directions

1. Combine broth, water, beans, onion, bay leaves and red pepper in slow cooker. Cover; cook on LOW 8 hours or on HIGH 4 hours.

2. Brown sausage in medium saucepan over medium heat, stirring to break up meat. Drain fat.

3. Add sausage, tomato, chili powder, Worcestershire sauce, oil, cumin and salt to slow cooker. Cover; cook on HIGH 15 minutes. Remove and discard bay leaves. Ladle soup into bowls; sprinkle with cilantro.   **Makes 9 servings**

country sausage and bean soup

Quick 'n' Easy

quick beef stew in foil

8 ounces boneless beef top sirloin steak, cut into 1-inch cubes

1 medium red potato, peeled and cut into ¾-inch cubes

1 cup frozen mixed vegetables

⅔ cup beef gravy

1 teaspoon minced fresh parsley

¼ teaspoon salt

¼ teaspoon dried thyme

⅛ teaspoon black pepper

1 sheet (20×12 inches) heavy-duty foil, lightly sprayed with nonstick cooking spray

1. Preheat oven to 450°F.

2. Combine beef, potato, vegetables, gravy, parsley, salt, thyme and black pepper in medium bowl; stir to mix.

3. Place beef mixture in center of foil sheet. Double fold sides and ends of foil to seal packet, leaving head space for heat circulation. Place packet on baking sheet.

4. Bake 30 minutes or until beef is tender. Carefully open one end of packet to allow steam to escape. Open packet and transfer stew to two bowls.   **Makes 2 servings**

quick and zesty vegetable soup

1 pound lean ground beef
½ cup chopped onion
   Salt and pepper
2 cans (14½ ounces each) DEL MONTE® Italian Recipe
   Stewed Tomatoes
2 cans (14 ounces each) beef broth
1 can (14½ ounces) DEL MONTE® Mixed Vegetables
½ cup uncooked medium egg noodles
½ teaspoon dried oregano

1. Brown meat with onion in large pot. Cook until onion is tender; drain. Season to taste with salt and pepper.

2. Stir in remaining ingredients. Bring to boil; reduce heat.

3. Cover and simmer 15 minutes or until noodles are tender.

Makes 8 servings

Prep Time: 5 minutes
Cook Time: 15 minutes

tip

A good soup pot is one that is heavy and conducts and distributes heat evenly. Copper is the ideal metal, though its cost puts it out of range for most cooks. Good alternatives are aluminum or stainless steel with a copper or aluminum core.

quick and zesty vegetable soup

chicken tortellini soup

6 cups chicken broth

1 package (9 ounces) refrigerated cheese and spinach tortellini

1 package (about 6 ounces) refrigerated fully cooked chicken breast strips, cut into bite-size pieces

2 cups baby spinach

4 to 6 tablespoons grated Parmesan cheese

1 tablespoon chopped fresh chives *or* 2 tablespoons sliced green onion

1. Bring broth to a boil in large saucepan over high heat; add tortellini. Reduce heat to medium; cook 5 minutes. Stir in chicken and spinach.

2. Reduce heat to low; cook 3 minutes or until chicken is heated through. Sprinkle with Parmesan cheese and chives.

Makes 4 servings

veg•all® black bean soup

1 package (14 ounces) smoked sausage, cut into ½-inch slices

2 cans (15 ounces each) VEG•ALL® Original Mixed Vegetables

2 cans (15 ounces each) black beans with spices, drained and rinsed

2 cans (14½ ounces) chicken broth

In large soup kettle, lightly brown sausage. Add Veg•All, beans and chicken broth; heat until hot. Serve immediately.

Makes 4 to 6 servings

chicken tortellini soup

beef stew in bread bowls

2 packages TYSON® Heat 'N Eat Beef Tips in Gravy*
2 cans (10.75 ounces each) vegetable and potato soup
2 tablespoons rosemary
4 large crusty hard rolls

*Look for TYSON® Heat 'N Eat Beef Tips in Gravy in your supermarket's refrigerated meat case.

1. Preheat oven to 325°F. Remove clear wrap and sleeves from trays of beef. Empty contents of bags into large ovenproof skillet.

2. Open cans of soup, strain juices from cans and add vegetables to beef. Mix well. Sprinkle rosemary over mixture.

3. Heat in oven 20 minutes or until contents are hot and steaming.

4. Using sharp knife, cut circle in top of rolls; remove tops and set aside. Pull bread center out to form bowls and set aside. Spoon hot stew into bread bowls. Serve top and interior bread pieces alongside stew for dipping. Refrigerate leftovers immediately. **Makes 4 servings**

Serving Suggestion: To add a little spice, sprinkle on a few red pepper flakes.

Prep Time: 5 minutes
Cook Time: 20 minutes
Total Time: 25 minutes

cream of asparagus soup

1 tablespoon margarine or butter
1 small onion, chopped
2 cans (14½ ounces each) chicken broth
1 jar (1 pound) RAGÚ® Cheesy!® Classic Alfredo Sauce
2 packages (10 ounces each) frozen asparagus spears, thawed

1. In 3½-quart saucepan, melt margarine over medium heat and cook onion, stirring occasionally, 5 minutes or until tender. Stir in broth, Ragú Cheesy! Sauce and asparagus. Bring to a boil over medium heat, stirring frequently. Reduce heat to low and simmer 5 minutes or until asparagus is tender.

2. In blender or food processor, purée hot soup mixture until smooth. Return soup to saucepan and heat through. Season, if desired, with salt and ground black pepper.

Makes 8 servings

Variation: For a Cream of Broccoli Soup, substitute frozen broccoli spears for asparagus.

Tip: Serve soup with cheese toast croutons. Simply place Swiss cheese on sliced French bread rounds and broil until cheese is melted.

Prep Time: 5 minutes
Cook Time: 20 minutes

ravioli soup

1 package (9 ounces) fresh or frozen cheese ravioli or tortellini

¾ pound hot Italian sausage, crumbled

1 can (14½ ounces) DEL MONTE® Italian Recipe Stewed Tomatoes

1 can (14¼ ounces) beef broth

1 can (14½ ounces) DEL MONTE® Cut Italian Green Beans, drained

2 green onions, sliced

1. Cook pasta according to package directions; drain.

2. Meanwhile, cook sausage in 5-quart pot over medium-high heat until no longer pink; drain. Add undrained tomatoes, broth and 1¾ cups water; bring to a boil.

3. Reduce heat to low; stir in pasta, beans and green onions. Simmer until heated through. Season with pepper and sprinkle with grated Parmesan cheese, if desired.   **Makes 4 servings**

Prep and Cook Time: 15 minutes

tip

Fresh filled pasta is very perishable; it must be refrigerated tightly wrapped and used within four to five days. Frozen filled pasta is available in most supermarkets. It can be stored frozen for up to four months. It should not be thawed before using, but cooked from the frozen state.

ravioli soup

all-in-one burger stew

1 pound ground beef
2 cups frozen Italian-style vegetables
1 can (about 14 ounces) diced tomatoes with basil and garlic
1 can (about 14 ounces) beef broth
2½ cups uncooked medium egg noodles
Salt and black pepper

1. Brown beef in Dutch oven or large skillet over medium-high heat 6 to 8 minutes, stirring to break up meat. Drain fat.

2. Add vegetables, tomatoes and broth; bring to a boil over high heat.

3. Add noodles; reduce heat to medium. Cover; cook 12 to 15 minutes or until noodles and vegetables are tender. Season with salt and pepper. **Makes 6 servings**

Note: For a special touch, sprinkle with chopped fresh parsley before serving.

Tip: To complete this meal, serve with breadsticks or a loaf of Italian bread and a simple salad.

Prep and Cook Time: 25 minutes

all-in-one burger stew

broccoli, cheese and rice soup

- 2 cups MINUTE® White or Brown Rice, uncooked
- 1 package (10 ounces) frozen chopped broccoli, thawed
- 1 can (10¾ ounces) reduced-fat cream of mushroom soup
- 3 cups low-fat milk
- 1 pound low-fat processed cheese, cubed
  Shredded cheese (optional)

Prepare rice according to package directions.

Combine broccoli, soup and milk in medium saucepan. Bring to simmer over medium heat.

Add cheese and stir until melted. Remove from heat and stir in rice. Top with shredded cheese, if desired.   **Makes 6 servings**

quick & easy meatball soup

- 1 package (15 to 18 ounces) frozen Italian sausage meatballs without sauce
- 2 cans (about 14 ounces each) Italian-style stewed tomatoes
- 2 cans (about 14 ounces each) beef broth
- 1 can (about 14 ounces) mixed vegetables
- ½ cup uncooked rotini pasta or small macaroni
- ½ teaspoon dried oregano

1. Thaw meatballs in microwave according to package directions.

2. Place remaining ingredients in large saucepan. Add meatballs; bring to a boil. Reduce heat; cover and simmer 15 minutes or until pasta is tender.   **Makes 4 to 6 servings**

broccoli, cheese and rice soup

quick broccoli soup

  4 cups chicken or vegetable broth,
    plus additional for thinning
2½ pounds broccoli florets
  1 onion, quartered
  1 cup milk
  ¼ cup crumbed blue cheese

1. Place broth, broccoli and onion in large saucepan; bring to a boil over high heat. Reduce heat to low; cover and simmer about 20 minutes or until vegetables are tender.

2. Purée soup in blender; return to saucepan. Add milk and additional broth, if necessary. Ladle soup into serving bowls; sprinkle with cheese.   **Makes 6 servings**

wild rice soup

  ½ cup dried lentils, rinsed and sorted
  1 package (6 ounces) long grain and wild rice blend
  1 can (about 14 ounces) vegetable broth
  1 package (10 ounces) frozen mixed vegetables
  1 cup milk
  2 slices (1 ounce each) American cheese, cut into pieces

1. Place lentils in small saucepan; cover with about 3 cups water. Bring to a boil. Reduce heat to low; cover and simmer 5 minutes. Let stand, covered, 1 hour. Drain and rinse lentils.

2. Cook rice according to package directions in medium saucepan. Add lentils, broth, vegetables, milk and cheese; bring to a boil. Reduce heat to low. Simmer, uncovered, 20 minutes.
                    Makes 6 servings

quick broccoli soup

Great-Tasting Poultry

country noodle soup

1 tablespoon I CAN'T BELIEVE IT'S NOT BUTTER!®
Spread
¼ cup finely chopped onion
½ cup finely chopped red bell pepper
2½ cups water
4 cups chicken broth or bouillon
1 package KNORR® PASTA SIDES™-Chicken Broccoli or
Chicken
½ cup cut-up cooked chicken, turkey or ham (optional)

Melt Spread in 4-quart saucepan over medium-high heat and
cook onion and red pepper, stirring occasionally, 5 minutes or
until tender. Stir in water and chicken broth. Bring just to a boil
over high heat. Stir in KNORR® PASTA SIDES™-Chicken Broccoli.
Continue boiling over medium heat, stirring occasionally,
8 minutes or until pasta is tender. Stir in chicken; heat through.

Makes 6 servings

Prep Time: 10 minutes
Cook Time: 16 minutes

baked bean stew

1 cup chopped onion
1 cup chopped green pepper
1 tablespoon vegetable oil
12 ounces boneless skinless chicken breast or tenders, cut into ½-inch pieces
2 cans (15 ounces each) baked beans or pork and beans
1 can (15 ounces) garbanzo beans or black-eyes or 1½ cups cooked dry-packaged garbanzo beans or black-eyes, rinsed, drained
1 can (14½ ounces) diced tomatoes with roasted garlic, undrained
¾ teaspoon dried sage leaves
½ teaspoon ground cumin
Salt and pepper, to taste

1. Cook onion and green pepper in oil in large saucepan until tender, 3 to 4 minutes. Add chicken and cook over medium heat until browned, 3 to 4 minutes.

2. Add beans, tomatoes and herbs to saucepan; heat to boiling. Reduce heat and simmer, uncovered, 8 to 10 minutes. Season to taste with salt and pepper.   **Makes 8 servings**

Tip: Frozen chopped onion and green pepper can be used. Stew can be prepared 1 to 2 days in advance; refrigerate, covered. Stew can also be frozen up to 2 months.

*Favorite recipe from **American Dry Bean Board***

baked bean stew

country turkey and veggie soup with cream

      2 tablespoons butter, divided
      8 ounces sliced mushrooms
      ½ cup chopped onion
      ½ cup thinly sliced celery
      1 red bell pepper, chopped
      1 carrot, thinly sliced
      ½ teaspoon dried thyme
      4 cups chicken or turkey broth
      4 ounces uncooked egg noodles
      2 cups chopped cooked turkey
      1 cup half-and-half
      ½ cup frozen peas, thawed
      ¾ teaspoon salt

Slow Cooker Directions

1. Melt 1 tablespoon butter in large nonstick skillet over medium-high heat. Add mushrooms and onion; cook and stir 4 minutes or until onion is translucent. Transfer mixture to slow cooker.

2. Add celery, bell pepper, carrot and thyme to slow cooker; pour in broth. Cover; cook on HIGH 2½ hours.

3. Add noodles and turkey. Cover; cook 20 minutes. Stir in half-and-half, peas, remaining 1 tablespoon butter and salt. Cook until noodles are tender and soup is heated through.

Makes 8 servings

country turkey and veggie soup with cream

hearty one-pot chicken stew

12 TYSON® Individually Frozen Boneless Skinless Chicken Tenderloins
1 box traditional red beans and rice mix
2¼ cups water
1 can (14.5 ounces) diced tomatoes, undrained
3 new red potatoes, unpeeled, cut into 1-inch pieces
2 carrots, sliced ½ inch thick
1 onion, cut into 1-inch pieces

1. Wash hands. Remove protective ice glaze from frozen chicken by holding under cool running water 1 to 2 minutes. Cut into 1-inch pieces. Wash hands.

2. In large saucepan, combine chicken, beans and rice, contents of seasoning packet, water, tomatoes, potatoes, carrots and onion. Bring to a boil. Cover, reduce heat; simmer 20 minutes or until internal juices of chicken run clear. (Or insert instant-read meat thermometer into thickest part of chicken. Temperature should read 180°F.) Refrigerate leftovers immediately.   **Makes 4 servings**

Serving Suggestions: Serve with hot rolls and a salad of mixed greens.

Prep Time: 10 minutes
Cook Time: 20 to 25 minutes

hearty one-pot chicken stew

chicken stew with dumplings

Chicken Stew

  2 tablespoons vegetable oil

  2 cups sliced carrots

  1 cup chopped onion

  1 large green bell pepper, sliced

  ½ cup sliced celery

  2 cans (about 14 ounces each) chicken broth, divided

  ¼ cup plus 2 tablespoons all-purpose flour

  2 pounds boneless skinless chicken breasts, cut into 1-inch pieces

  3 medium potatoes, unpeeled and cut into 1-inch pieces

  6 ounces mushrooms, halved

  ¾ cup frozen peas

  1 teaspoon dried basil

  ¾ teaspoon dried rosemary

  ¼ teaspoon dried tarragon

  ¾ to 1 teaspoon salt

  ¼ teaspoon black pepper

Herb Dumplings

  2 cups biscuit baking mix

  ½ teaspoon dried basil

  ½ teaspoon dried rosemary

  ¼ teaspoon dried tarragon

  ⅔ cup milk

1. For chicken stew, heat oil in 4-quart Dutch oven over medium heat. Add carrots, onion, bell pepper and celery; cook and stir 5 minutes or until onion is tender. Reserve ½ cup broth. Stir remaining broth into vegetable mixture; bring to a boil. Mix

reserved ½ cup broth and flour in small bowl; stir into boiling mixture. Boil, stirring constantly, 1 minute or until thickened. Stir chicken, potatoes, mushrooms, peas and herbs into mixture. Reduce heat to low; simmer, covered, 18 to 20 minutes or until vegetables are almost tender and chicken is cooked through. Add salt and black pepper.

2. For herb dumplings, combine biscuit mix and herbs in small bowl; stir in milk to form soft dough. Evenly spoon dumpling mixture on top of stew in 8 large spoonfuls. Cook, uncovered, 10 minutes. Cover and cook 10 minutes or until dumplings are tender and toothpick inserted into centers comes out clean.

Makes 8 servings

Make-Ahead Time: up to 2 days before serving
Final Prep and Cook Time: 30 minutes

country stew

>   **2 bags SUCCESS® Brown Rice**
>   **1 pound ground turkey**
>   **1 small onion, chopped**
>   **2 cans (14½ ounces each) tomatoes, cut-up, undrained**
>   **1 teaspoon pepper**
> **½ teaspoon dried basil leaves, crushed**
> **½ teaspoon garlic powder**
>   **1 can (16 ounces) whole kernel corn, drained**

Prepare rice according to package directions.

Brown ground turkey with onion in large skillet, stirring occasionally to separate turkey. Add tomatoes, pepper, basil and garlic powder; simmer 20 minutes, stirring occasionally. Stir in rice and corn; heat thoroughly, stirring occasionally.

Makes 8 servings

chicken rotini soup

½ **pound boneless skinless chicken breasts, cut into ½-inch pieces**
1 **cup water**
2 **tablespoons butter**
½ **medium onion, chopped**
4 **ounces mushrooms, sliced**
4 **cups chicken broth**
1 **teaspoon Worcestershire sauce**
¼ **teaspoon dried tarragon**
¾ **cup uncooked rotini pasta**
1 **small zucchini, thinly sliced**

1. Combine chicken and water in medium saucepan; bring to a boil over high heat. Reduce heat to medium-low; simmer 2 minutes. Drain water and rinse chicken.

2. Melt butter in 5-quart Dutch oven or large saucepan over medium heat. Add onion and mushrooms; cook and stir until onion is tender. Stir in chicken, broth, Worcestershire sauce and tarragon; bring to a boil over high heat. Stir in pasta. Reduce heat to medium-low; simmer, uncovered, 5 minutes.

3. Add zucchini to soup; simmer, uncovered, 5 minutes or until pasta is tender.   **Makes 4 servings**

chicken rotini soup

turkey vegetable rice soup

1½ pounds turkey drumsticks (2 small)
8 cups cold water
1 medium onion, cut into quarters
2 tablespoons soy sauce
¼ teaspoon black pepper
1 bay leaf
2 medium carrots, sliced
⅓ cup uncooked rice
4 ounces mushrooms, sliced
1 cup snow peas
1 cup coarsely chopped bok choy

1. Place turkey in 5-quart Dutch oven. Add water, onion, soy sauce, pepper and bay leaf; bring to a boil over high heat. Reduce heat to medium-low; simmer, uncovered, 1½ hours or until turkey is tender.

2. Remove turkey from Dutch oven; let broth cool slightly. Skim fat; discard bay leaf. Remove turkey meat from bones; discard skin and bones. Cut turkey into bite-size pieces.

3. Add carrots and rice to broth in Dutch oven; bring to a boil over high heat. Reduce heat to medium-low; simmer, uncovered, 10 minutes.

4. Add mushrooms and turkey to soup; bring to a boil over high heat. Reduce heat to medium-low; simmer, uncovered, 5 minutes.

5. Cut snow peas in half crosswise. Stir snow peas and bok choy into soup; bring to a boil over high heat. Reduce heat to medium-low; simmer, uncovered, 8 minutes or until rice and vegetables are tender. **Makes 6 servings**

turkey vegetable rice soup

chunky chicken vegetable soup

- **1 teaspoon vegetable oil**
- **½ pound boneless skinless chicken breasts, cut into ½-inch cubes**
- **1 can (14½ ounces) chicken broth**
- **2 cups water**
- **2 cups assorted cut-up vegetables (sliced carrots, broccoli florets, chopped red bell pepper)***
- **1 packet Italian salad dressing and recipe mix**
- **1 cup MINUTE® White Rice, uncooked**
- **2 tablespoons fresh parsley, chopped**

Or substitute 1 package (10 ounces) frozen mixed vegetables, thawed.

Heat oil in large saucepan over medium-high heat. Add chicken; cook and stir until browned.

Add broth, water, vegetables and salad dressing mix. Bring to a boil. Reduce heat to low; cover. Simmer 5 minutes.

Stir in rice and parsley; cover. Remove from heat. Let stand 5 minutes.   **Makes 4 servings**

tip

Thoroughly wash cutting surfaces, utensils and your hands with hot soapy water after coming in contact with uncooked chicken. This eliminates the risk of contaminating other foods with salmonella bacteria that is often present in raw chicken. Salmonella is killed during cooking.

slow-cooked chicken and mushroom stew

4 TYSON® Individually Frozen Boneless Skinless Chicken Breasts

1 can (10.75 ounces) cream of mushroom and roasted garlic soup

Salt and black pepper, to taste

8 ounces medium white mushrooms

1 cup baby-cut carrots

2 celery ribs, cut into 1½-inch lengths

Slow Cooker Directions

1. Stir together soup and ½ can of water in slow cooker. Wash hands. Cut chicken into 2-inch chunks. Sprinkle with salt and pepper to taste. Put chicken in slow cooker. Wash hands. Add mushrooms, carrots and celery. Stir gently to mix.

2. Cover and cook on LOW 6 to 8 hours or until internal juices of chicken run clear. (Or insert instant-read meat thermometer into thickest part of chicken. Temperature should read 180°F.) Refrigerate leftovers immediately.　　　**Makes 4 servings**

Serving Suggestion: Serve with rice sprinkled with parsley.

Prep Time: 10 minutes
Cook Time: 6 to 8 hours (LOW)

Homestyle Vegetarian

slow cooker veggie stew

1 tablespoon vegetable oil
⅔ cup carrot slices
½ cup diced onion
2 cloves garlic, chopped
2 cans (about 14 ounces each) vegetable broth
1½ cups chopped green cabbage
½ cup cut green beans
½ cup diced zucchini
1 tablespoon tomato paste
½ teaspoon dried basil
½ teaspoon dried oregano
¼ teaspoon salt

Slow Cooker Directions

1. Heat oil in medium skillet over medium-high heat. Add carrot, onion and garlic; cook and stir until tender.

2. Place carrot mixture and remaining ingredients in slow cooker; stir to combine. Cover; cook on LOW 8 to 10 hours or on HIGH 4 to 5 hours. **Makes 4 to 6 servings**

fresh lime and black bean soup

2 cans (about 15 ounces each) black beans, undrained
1 can (about 14 ounces) vegetable broth
1½ cups chopped onions
1½ teaspoons chili powder
¾ teaspoon ground cumin
¼ teaspoon garlic powder
⅛ to ¼ teaspoon red pepper flakes
½ cup sour cream
2 tablespoons extra virgin olive oil
2 tablespoons chopped fresh cilantro
1 medium lime, cut into wedges

Slow Cooker Directions

1. Coat slow cooker with nonstick cooking spray. Add beans, broth, onions, chili powder, cumin, garlic powder and red pepper flakes. Cover; cook on LOW 7 hours or on HIGH 3½ hours.

2. To thicken soup, place half of soup mixture in food processor or blender; process until smooth. Stir into remaining soup in slow cooker. Let stand 15 to 20 minutes before serving.

3. Serve soup with sour cream, oil, cilantro and lime wedges.

Makes 4 servings

Prep Time: 10 minutes
Cook Time: 7 hours (LOW) or 3½ hours (HIGH)

fresh lime and black bean soup

chickpea and orange squash stew

1 teaspoon canola oil

¾ cup chopped onion

½ to 1 jalapeño pepper,* seeded and minced

1 (½-inch) piece fresh ginger, peeled and minced

1 clove garlic, minced

2 teaspoons ground cumin

½ teaspoon ground coriander

1 cup cubed peeled orange squash, sweet potato or
    pumpkin

1 cup canned chickpeas, rinsed and drained

½ cup water

1½ teaspoons soy sauce

1 cup coconut milk

Juice of 1 lime

¼ cup chopped fresh cilantro

Spinach leaves (optional)

Jalapeño peppers can sting and irritate the skin, so wear rubber gloves when handling peppers and do not touch your eyes.

1. Heat oil in medium saucepan over medium-low heat. Add onion, jalapeño pepper, ginger and garlic; cook and stir 2 to 3 minutes or until onion is translucent. Add cumin and coriander; cook and stir 1 minute.

2. Add squash, chickpeas, water and soy sauce to saucepan; bring to a boil. Reduce heat and simmer 15 minutes or until squash is tender. Add coconut milk; cook and stir 2 to 3 minutes or until heated through. Stir in lime juice and cilantro. Garnish with spinach. **Makes 2 servings**

chickpea and orange squash stew

italian hillside garden soup

1 tablespoon olive oil
1 cup chopped onion
1 cup chopped green bell pepper
½ cup sliced celery
2 cans (about 14 ounces each) vegetable broth
1 can (about 15 ounces) navy beans, rinsed and
    drained
1 can (about 14 ounces) diced tomatoes with basil,
    garlic and oregano
1 medium zucchini, chopped
1 cup frozen cut green beans, thawed
¼ teaspoon garlic powder
1 package (9 ounces) refrigerated cheese tortellini
3 tablespoons chopped fresh basil
    Grated Asiago or Parmesan cheese (optional)

Slow Cooker Directions

1. Heat oil in large skillet over medium-high heat. Add onion, bell pepper and celery; cook and stir 4 minutes or until onion is translucent. Transfer to slow cooker.

2. Add broth, navy beans, tomatoes, zucchini, green beans and garlic powder. Cover; cook on LOW 7 hours or on HIGH 3½ hours.

3. Turn slow cooker to HIGH. Add tortellini; cook 20 minutes or until pasta is tender. Stir in basil. Sprinkle with cheese just before serving.   **Makes 6 servings**

Prep Time: 15 minutes
Cook Time: 7 hours (LOW) or 3½ hours (HIGH)

italian hillside garden soup

lentil stew over couscous

3 cups dried lentils (1 pound), sorted and rinsed
3 cups water
1 can (about 14 ounces) vegetable broth
1 can (about 14 ounces) diced tomatoes
1 large onion, chopped
1 green bell pepper, chopped
4 stalks celery, chopped
1 medium carrot, halved lengthwise and sliced
2 cloves garlic, chopped
1 teaspoon dried marjoram
¼ teaspoon black pepper
1 tablespoon olive oil
1 tablespoon cider vinegar
4½ to 5 cups hot cooked couscous

Slow Cooker Directions

1. Combine lentils, water, broth, tomatoes, onion, bell pepper, celery, carrot, garlic, marjoram and black pepper in slow cooker; stir. Cover; cook on LOW 8 to 9 hours.

2. Stir in oil and vinegar. Serve over couscous.

Makes 12 servings

Tip: Lentil stew keeps well in the refrigerator for up to 1 week. Stew can also be frozen in an airtight container for up to 3 months.

Prep Time: 10 minutes
Cook Time: 8 to 9 hours

lentil stew over couscous

curried sweet potato and carrot soup

    2 sweet potatoes, peeled and cut into ¾-inch cubes
       (about 5 cups)
    2 cups baby carrots
    1 onion, chopped
    ¾ teaspoon curry powder
    ½ teaspoon salt
    ½ teaspoon ground cinnamon
    ½ teaspoon black pepper
    ¼ teaspoon ground ginger
    4 cups vegetable broth
    ¾ cup half-and-half
    1 tablespoon maple syrup
       Candied ginger (optional)

Slow Cooker Directions

1. Place sweet potatoes, carrots, onion, curry powder, salt, cinnamon, pepper and ground ginger in slow cooker. Add broth; stir well to combine. Cover; cook on LOW 7 to 8 hours.

2. Working in batches, process soup in food processor or blender until smooth. Return to slow cooker. Add half-and-half and maple syrup. Cover; cook on HIGH 15 minutes or until heated through. Garnish with candied ginger.   **Makes 8 servings**

Prep Time: 10 minutes
Cook Time: 7 to 8 hours

curried sweet potato and carrot soup

mushroom barley stew

- 1 tablespoon olive oil
- 1 medium onion, finely chopped
- 1 cup chopped carrots (about 2 carrots)
- 1 clove garlic, minced
- 5 cups vegetable broth
- 1 cup uncooked pearl barley
- 1 cup dried wild mushrooms, broken into pieces
- 1 teaspoon salt
- ½ teaspoon dried thyme
- ½ teaspoon black pepper

Slow Cooker Directions

1. Heat oil in medium skillet over medium-high heat. Add onion, carrots and garlic; cook and stir 5 minutes or until tender. Place in slow cooker.

2. Add broth, barley, mushrooms, salt, thyme and pepper to slow cooker; stir well to combine.

3. Cover; cook on LOW 6 to 7 hours.   **Makes 4 to 6 servings**

Variation: To turn this thick, robust stew into a soup, add 2 to 3 additional cups of broth. Cook the same length of time.

Prep Time: 10 minutes
Cook Time: 6 to 7 hours

mushroom barley stew

Index

Acknowledgments

The publisher would like to thank the companies and organizations listed below for the use of their recipes and photographs in this publication.

Del Monte Foods

Riviana Foods Inc.

Tyson Foods, Inc.

Unilever

US Dry Bean Council

Veg•All®